Sunshine Through the Pain

Beverly J. Scott

BK Royston Publishing
P. O. Box 4321
Jeffersonville, IN 47131
502-802-5385
http://www.bkroystonpublishing.com
bkroystonpublishing@gmail.com

© Copyright 2022

All Rights Reserved. No part of this book may be reproduced, stored in a retrieval system, or transmitted by any means without the written permission of the author.

Cover Design: Elite Book Covers
Back Cover Photo: Beverly Scott
Additional Drawings: Chance Lee, Sr.

ISBN-13: 978-1-955063-66-1

Printed in the United States of America

Dedication

I dedicate this book of poems to my mother my rock Julia Aline Thompson a wise woman and a true Queen.......

Table of Contents

Dedication

Don't Waste A Day!	1
The Sea Speaks To Me!	5
Candle	9
Love	13
Mother's Day Card	17
Row Me Oh Lord,	21
Peace Be Still	23
What this Rose Means to Me	27
Thank You, God	31
Broken Vein	35
The Snake, God Could Not Take!	37
God's Mercy	43
Family	45
Prepare the Way of the Lord	47
The Sea Speaks to Me	51
About the Author	55

Don't Waste A Day!

Don't waste a day, although you're not where you want to be, Travel Far deep within, don't waste a day forget about those so-called friends, no matter what they say, You're future bright, you're the pilot of your own flight! So set the course, and aim that Plane! You're headed for wisdom, purpose, peace, and if you stop wasting a day, you have only your own to blame! Think of things that haven't been done, Press those gears to the kingdom, Come! Don't waste a day! You have a gift and a story that might be told! If not, you're a star in God's show!

Reflection

Reflection

The Sea Speaks To Me!

I walk along the beach, and I look to the sea, a voice whisper to me, This life you live is not your own you're not walking and talking alone! So pace yourself don't run too fast. This journey of yours will last and last! Your Cries I hear, there's no need to fear. Dry your eyes and stop those tears. There's no need to weep your faith is so deep. I know at times you cannot sleep, but that's alright walk with me to the sea there's a shell, I put it there! Pick it up! Now smell the air! See those Dove flying high just like you, they won't stop until they reach the other side! So pace yourself don't run too fast, this beach of yours will last and last.

Reflection

Reflection

Candle

The flames burn so brightly within, it takes me so far to where my life begins, I lie and think and look at the flames, it makes me think who was the blame, so deep inside the light it burns, and rises up with much concern. It takes me out of this body of mind it enlightens, it twinkles pure divine. The light shines, but not too bright it's just enough light to meditate at night. No matter how many I light, they're all the same. I know these is God's heavenly things! I've searched and searched the entire core and come with wisdom and Oh so much more! I thank you for this candle of mind, and one day to be just as divine!

Reflection

Reflection

_____
_____
_____
_____
_____
_____
_____
_____
_____
_____
_____
_____
_____
_____
_____
_____
_____
_____
_____
_____

Love

If only I could speak! This is what I would say! "Oh, so many of you have hurt and abused me, in so many ways! You started to care, you were sweet, compassionate, helpful, and strong. Loves are not supposed to hurt or cause pain. You took this Love and turn it into a game! A little give a little take, a little sacrifice, that's my name! To be there for me, like I was for you, to show me respect and give the help when needed to talk to listen. The next time you used the name Love and expect me to do the same, make sure you know how

to play the love game.

Reflection

Reflection

_____
_____
_____
_____
_____
_____
_____
_____
_____
_____
_____
_____
_____
_____
_____
_____
_____
_____
_____
_____
_____

Mother's Day Card

I know what you've been through this year, I know how you've stood still, through it all! I know the tears you've cried and you still held on with God at your side! I know the walks, you've walked. I know the treads of your tires; I know the pain you felt. I know the financial state you were in when the snowmelt! I know all this because I was there, and you never stopped or complain. You keep on going even in the rain! A brought card can't explain, it doesn't feel, it hasn't seen, can't touch words, can't be told, because you see it was me, with

you on that same road!

Reflection

Reflection

Row Me Oh Lord,

Row me Oh Lord, Row me Oh Lord! Like you rowed the scrolls, Please un-row me from head to toe! Read my body Oh Lord, touch my soul! Give me Wisdom and knowledge let your words flow! I realize Lord it could have been me instead of Job! My father's rich in houses, and land he holds the keys to my heavenly plans, Hold me Oh Lord, and fold my hands, keep me on my knees so I can pray and pray, as I flow through this land! This body is yours and time will tell, you see I am the woman at the well.

Reflection

Peace Be Still

As I lie here trembling inside knowing not which way my soul desires, I realize the Ocean's waves inside, casting floods of rivers and all the waters, my soul desires, "Peace be still" it chants to my heart, ache no more for your life, I'll move to depart! You've shown me what God created in you, It has helped me understand the people that are true, I had my doubt but the spirit that you cast keeps me working and creating until the last, so winds flow on and Ocean's runs and Peace be still because you're on your own shore! You're his child without a doubt so,

Whenever you think I'm not near, just move those oceans of pain and tears. You are casting me from side to side. Keep praising God because He's the Most High, no matter what they say, are what goes on God! He'll make them leave you alone! And you're his child and I am proud to say, he created for you the perfect fight. I know it gets hard but that's alright! Peace be still for I've had a wonderful life!

Reflection

Reflection

What this Rose Means to Me

As the rose begins to open, I opened my home to you. I opened my heart to you. Understanding each other wasn't easy. I didn't think it would be so I closed my heart back up. The petals fell I begin to pray. The first petal was for acceptance. The second petal was for knowledge, the third petal was for peace. The fourth petal was for courage. All these things you have shown to me. My heart beats at a different pace now. I realize I didn't need to open my heart. All I needed was for you, to be apart.

Reflection

Reflection

Thank You, God

Thank you, God for being my enabler, enabling me to maintain, giving me the power to deal with what may come my way! No matter how many times, I've fallen you still called my name, pick me up, and said "My child you will never taste hell! You're mine so get up and start again! No matter what you are going through I'll be there! You have given me a taste of what's fine. You have hailed me to the highest through generations and times though your family and friends sometimes left you alone, this was good, it gives you time to write and talk to me, and be your own. You to write and talk to me and be on your own. To grow and grow and turn into a beautiful rose! You are mine and I am your enabler. You are part of my soul.

Reflection

Reflection

Broken Vein

Lord heal this vein deep within that helps eases the pain, There's thousands of them between muscles and bones, and skin that's thin! But this view of mine lies deep within, it keeps me straight, when I want to sin. It keeps my sight and helps me to eat right this is the vein that controls the senses, It causes much pain, you see this is the vein, connected to brain!.

Reflection

The Snake, God Could Not Take!

God created the heavens and earth! God saw the light that it was good and divided the light from the darkness. He called the light day! And the darkness night!. This was the first day! The second day he created evening and mornings, On the third day God created the water under the heaven and gathered together unto one place, and let the dry land appear and he called it to earth! The waters were called the seas. On the fourth day, God let the herb yield seed and those were fruit trees! On the fifth day "God said, there be light in the fire of the heaven, to divide the day from the night, let them be for signs, four seasons and for the days and years, God made two great lights. The greater light rules the day, and the lesser light rules the night!

He also makes the stars. On the sixth day, God created all the moving creature's that moves all the animals of the waters and beast of the earth after his kind. He made man after His likeness to have dominion over the fish of the sea. The birds of the air, as over the cattle and over all the earth! Every creeping thing crept upon the earth. So He creates man in his own image. Then he created a female. On the seventh day God rested. God blessed the seventh day and sacrificed it, because in it He rested from all his work, which was created and made! God planted a garden eastward in Eden, and there he put the man, whom He formed out of the ground made the Lord God. The woman came out of the side of the man that the Lord God created. God grew every tree that is pleasant to the sight and good for food. The tree of life is in the midst of the garden, and the tree of knowledge of good and evil! God said to Adam and Eve, The Lord God commanded saying of every Tree of Garden, thou mayest freely eat! But of the tree of knowledge of good and evil, Thou shall not eat. For in the day that thou easiest thereof, Thou shall surely die! Now the serpent one of God's creations, One of the beasts of the fields, was more subtle than any other beast! The serpent tempted the woman, Eve in the garden and Eve said unto the serpent, "we may eat of the fruit of the trees which are in the midst of the garden, we shall not eat! Lest we die! For if we eat of it, Our eyes shall be opened, and we will be as gods knowing good and evil. But when Eve saw that the tree was good for food, and it was pleasant to the eyes, and a tree to be desired to make one wise which was a trick from the serpent, she took of the fruit, thereof and did eat. And gave also to Adam and the eyes of them both were opened. They looked at each other and knew that was the Snake, God could not take!!!

Reflection

God's Mercy

God's Mercy kept me so I wouldn't let go! I don't take this day or any day for granted! I thank God for another chance of life! He didn't have to do it, but He did! I will praise him every day, for another today! You may not understand, but when the doctor said, "She died!" But God said, "Oh no, she's alive, you see I have so much for her to do, and I will see her through!"

Reflection

Family

Love can sometimes be found, hurt can sometimes be repaired, sickness can be sometimes be well, smiles can sometimes turn to laughter, tears can be washed away, but words can never be replaced! And nothing worse than time, that has escaped! Be kind to one another because all these things you'll have to face it when you see God and reach that higher, heavenly place!

Reflection

Prepare the Way of the Lord

Prepare me, for my journey home, making myself ready.

I've got to be strong. Don't cry for me, please do the same, God had a plan for this journey of mine it's a beautiful thing. I had a good life I can't complain, God, placed my mother beside me in times when I had pain. I want her to know what she did was not vain! She prepared me well with the love she shared, so dry those tears and don't be afraid, I'll be with you always, especially on Mother's Day! The family has peace within your souls, from the beginning to the end, God's in control.

P.S In remembrance of my cousin Philip Malone who passed September 16, 2007, of Kidney Problems, Age 34

Reflection

Reflection

The Sea Speaks to Me

I walk along the beach, and I look to the sea, A voice whisper to me, This life you live is not your own, you're not walking and talking alone! So pace yourself. Don't run to fast, This journey of yours will last and last! Your cries are here, There's no need to fear. Dry your eyes and stop those tears! There's no need to weep, your faith is deep! I know at times you cannot sleep! But that alright walk with me too the sea! There's a shell, I put it there. Pick it up! Now smell the air! See those doves flying high just like you. They won't stop until they reach the other side! So pace yourself don't run too fast! This beach of yours will last and last!

Reflection

Reflection

About the Author

Born and raised in East Jefferson County Ky on my grandmothers farm, I learned all about farming life at an early age. My grandfather and grandmother Mr. & Mrs. Ben McAtee had nine children and a house full of grandchildren. We all lived in the house that my grandfather built. My mother Julia Aline Thompson had five children. Her sister Frankie Robinson had five children. The house was very full. We planted vegetables and had apple trees, pear trees and grapes to pick.

At the age of nine my mother married my step dad and we moved in the city of Louisville Kentucky. Growing up in the city was quite different, busy streets crowded stores. I attended Male High School, graduated and went to Jefferson State Community College. I also attended Watterson College and earned my degree at the School of Hair Design in Louisville Kentucky. I am a mother of two children Cassandra Simmons and Frederick Deon Simmons. I am a grandmother of one RaKim Johnell Nelson. I fostered and three children and raised seventy five children. I have an Associate of Arts Degree and Biblical Studies Degree. I am also a retired lead teacher for JCPS.

I have an online antique business called Aline's Attic Antiques ailenesantiques5.@godaddysites.com check it out! Nobody but God has made all this possible. My mom taught me this at an early age about the love of Jesus. With all the trials and tribulations that I have experienced this turning point of my life It was God at the beginning and it will be God at the end.

www.ingramcontent.com/pod-product-compliance
Lightning Source LLC
Chambersburg PA
CBHW031215090426

42736CB00009B/930